A Note to Parents

DK READERS is a compelling program for beginning readers, designed in conjunction with leading literacy experts, including Dr. Linda Gambrell, Distinguished Professor of Education at Clemson University. Dr. Gambrell has served as President of the National Reading Conference, the College Reading Association, and the International Reading Association.

Beautiful illustrations and superb full-color photographs combine with engaging, easy-to-read stories to offer a fresh approach to each subject in the series. Each DK READER is guaranteed to capture a child's interest while developing his or her reading skills, general knowledge, and love of reading.

The five levels of DK READERS are aimed at different reading abilities, enabling you to choose the books that are exactly right for your child:

Pre-level 1: Learning to read
Level 1: Beginning to read
Level 2: Beginning to read alone
Level 3: Reading alone
Level 4: Proficient readers

The "normal" age at which a child begins to read can be anywhere from three to eight years old. Adult participation through the lower levels is very helpful for providing encouragement, discussing storylines, and sounding out unfamiliar words.

No matter which level you select, you can be sure that you are helping your child learn to read, then read to learn!

Penguin
Random
House

For Dorling Kindersley
Project Editor Heather Scott
Designer Jon Hall
Senior Designer Ron Stobbart
Brand Manager Lisa Lanzarini
Publishing Manager Simon Beecroft
Category Publisher Alex Allan
Production Controller Jen Lockwood
Production Editor Siu Chan

For Lucasfilm
Executive Editor Jonathan W. Rinzler
Art Director Troy Alders
Continuity Supervisor Leland Chee
Director of Publishing Carol Roeder

Reading Consultant
Linda B. Gambrell, Ph.D

First published in the United States in 2009 by
DK Publishing
345 Hudson Street
New York, New York 10014

15 10 9 8 7 6 5 4 3 2
015-SD409—10/08

DK Books are available at special discounts when purchased in bulk
for sales promotions, premiums, fund-raising, or educational use. For
details, contact: DK Publishing Special Markets, 345 Hudson Street,
New York, New York 10014, SpecialSales@dk.com

Published in Great Britain by Dorling Kindersley Limited.
A catalog record for this book is available from the Library of
Congress

ISBN: 978-0-7566-4517-5 (Hardback)
ISBN: 978-0-7566-4516-8 (Paperback)

Color reproduction by MDP
Printed and bound by L Rex, China

A WORLD OF IDEAS:
SEE ALL THERE IS TO KNOW

Contents

4   R2-D2

6   Droid Jobs

8   Special Powers

10   Deadly Missions

12   Astromech Droids

14   C-3PO

16   Clumsy Droid

18   Famous Adventures

20   Protocol Droids

22   Droids Everywhere

24   Medical Droids

26   Deadly Droids

28   Spy Droids

30   One of a Kind

32   Test your Knowledge

DK READERS

STAR WARS

BEGINNING
TO READ ALONE
2

R2-D2
AND FRIENDS

Written by Simon Beecroft

R2-D2

R2-D2

This is R2-D2. He is a clever machine called a droid.

R2-D2 talks using whistles and beeps. He can talk to other droids, and some humans can understand him as well.

R2-D2 is not very big, but he is no pushover. When he is angry, he bounces up and down and stamps his feet!

Droid height
R2-D2 is just under one meter tall. R2-D2 is only a little bit shorter than Anakin when he was a young boy.

Droid Jobs

R2-D2 is an astromech droid.
Astromech droids take care of
spaceships. Sometimes they
help human pilots fly
spaceships, too.

*R2-D2 helped
Anakin to fly
this spaceship.*

R2-D2 can talk to computers that help fly the spaceships. He plugs a special tool into the computer to talk to it.

R2-D2 has lots of tools hidden inside his body. So don't be surprised if a cutting arm or a grasping arm pops out of a panel in his body.

Special Powers

R2-D2 moves around on his three wheeled feet. R2-D2 can fly as well. He uses rocket boosters that pop out of his sides.

Secret message

R2-D2 can record and play messages. Here's Princess Leia, who recorded a secret message for Obi-Wan Kenobi.

R2-D2 can look around corners or from underwater using a special eye that pops up from the top of his head.

Deadly Missions

R2-D2's life is very exciting.

He once repaired Padmé Amidala's spaceship from the outside while it was flying in space.

Owners

R2-D2 has worked for Padmé Amidala, Anakin Skywalker, Princess Leia, and Luke Skywalker.

Another time, some Jawas captured R2-D2. The Jawas sold R2-D2 to Owen Lars, Luke Skywalker's uncle.

R4-G9   R5-X2   R4-A22

Astromech Droids

Astromech droids like R2-D2 come
in all sorts of colors and styles.

R2-D2 used to work
with a team of
astromech droids in
Padmé Amidala's
spaceship.

R4-P17 had a red dome. The droid
was built into Obi-Wan Kenobi's
spaceship. Unfortunately a nasty
buzz droid destroyed R4-P17 in
a big space battle.

Uncle Owen nearly
bought a droid called
R5-D4. But it was faulty
and its head blew up. So
Owen chose trusty R2-D2 instead.

R5-D4

C-3PO

R2-D2 is best friends with a golden droid called C-3PO. R2-D2 is scared of nothing, but C-3PO worries about everything!

C-3PO is a protocol droid. Protocol droids can speak millions of languages. They help people in the galaxy speak to each other.

See-through PO!

Anakin Skywalker built C-3PO. At first, C-3PO was not covered in shiny golden metal. You could see all his wires and parts. C-3PO said that he felt naked!

Clumsy Droid

Parts of C-3PO's body would sometimes fall off. Luckily, it doesn't hurt him and he can be repaired.

Once, a big machine in a factory pulled off C-3PO's head by mistake. The machine put a battle droid's head onto his body. Luckily, R2-D2 came to C-3PO's rescue!

R2-D2 puts C-3PO's correct head back on.

Another time, C-3PO was completely taken apart. If it hadn't been for his friend Chewbacca, he'd have been recycled!

Clean machine
C-3PO loves to soak in an oil bath. It cleans off all the dust and dirt from his parts and makes him feel like new again.

Famous Adventures

C-3PO and R2-D2 have had lots of adventures together!

They once traveled to Jabba the Hutt's palace to rescue their friend Han Solo. But Jabba captured them. Jabba forced C-3PO to become his translator droid. Poor R2-D2 became a waiter, with a drinks tray attached to his head!

On another mission, C-3PO met the furry Ewoks, who live in tree houses. The Ewoks thought that such a shiny droid must have great magical powers!

Protocol Droids

Most protocol droids are friendly, but some are dangerous.

TC-14 tried to trick Qui-Gon Jinn and Obi-Wan Kenobi. She led them into a room that filled with poisonous gas.
The Jedi escaped and they let TC-14 go.

TC-14 looks like C-3PO, but she is silver not gold.

4-LOM has a body like C-3PO, but his head is shaped like an insect's head. His job is to capture people. Darth Vader

4-LOM

once wanted him to find and capture Han Solo.

CZ-3

CZ-3 was an unlucky droid. He got mixed up in one of Jabba the Hutt's criminal plots. He was destroyed and scrap dealers stole his remains.

Droids Everywhere

Droids are everywhere. They do all sorts of jobs.

This gatekeeper droid stands inside the door at Jabba's palace. When visitors knock, it pokes its eye through a peep-hole in the door.

Gonk, gonk! What's that noise? It's a GNK droid, also called a gonk droid. Gonk droids walk around on two legs and supply power to machines.

Gonk droid

Watch out for MSE-6 droids, also called mouse droids. These small cleaning and repair droids whiz by your feet—don't trip over one!

Mouse droid

Medical Droids

If you are ill or hurt, you might need a medical droid to take care of you!

A team of medical droids rebuilt Darth Vader's body after he was hurt in a fight with Obi-Wan Kenobi. They fitted black armor and a black helmet onto his body.

A medical droid called
2-1B treated Luke
Skywalker after he was
lost in the snow. 2-1B
also fitted Luke with a
mechanical hand after he lost his
own in a fight with Darth Vader.

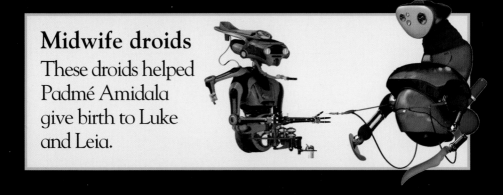

Midwife droids
These droids helped
Padmé Amidala
give birth to Luke
and Leia.

Deadly Droids

Some droids, such as battle droids, are not friendly. They have blasters and other deadly weapons.

Droidekas roll into battle like a ball. Then they

Battle droid

Droideka

unwind and shield themselves in energy. They have blasters on both arms.

Spider droids walk on four legs. Their dome-shaped heads are

Spider droid

fitted with cannons that blast at anything in their path.

Droid starfighters can fly in space, with their guns blazing. They can also walk into battle on the tips of their wings. Either way, watch out!

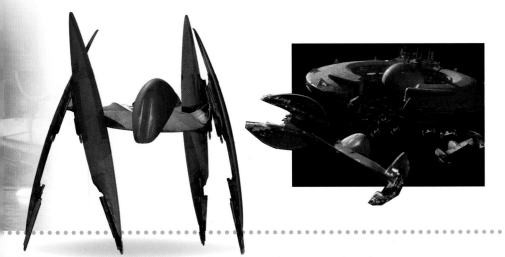

Spy Droids

Spy droids might be watching you so beware!

Darth Maul's spy droids fly around looking for Queen Amidala, Jedi Qui-Gon Jinn, and Obi-Wan Kenobi.

Spy droid

Darth Vader used probe droids to look for his enemies. Han Solo destroyed this one with his blaster!

Imperial droids

Little patrol droids are everywhere, looking for criminals. They report to Stormtroopers.

One of a Kind

If anything attacks R2-D2, he has some surprises in store! He can frighten off attackers by shooting out jets of smoke and making loud noises and whistles.

Once he destroyed a deadly buzz droid that attacked Anakin Skywalker's spaceship!

But R2-D2 won't frighten you.
You are one of his friends. Listen.
"Beep whoot ooo!" R2-D2 is saying
goodbye to you.

Goodbye, R2-D2!

Test your Knowledge

Which of these droids are friendly and which are not?

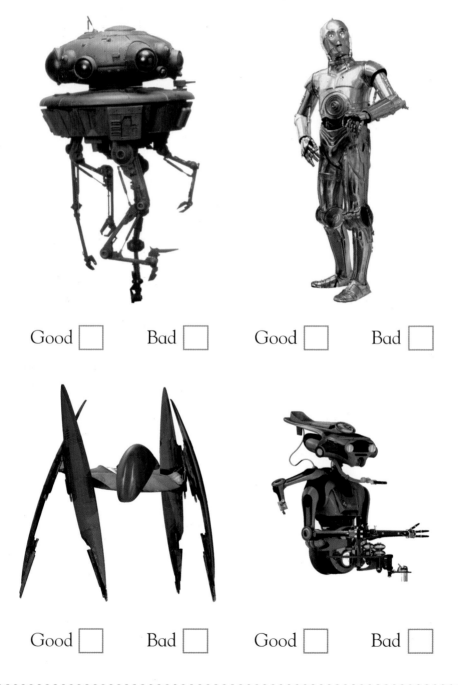

Good ☐   Bad ☐   Good ☐   Bad ☐

Good ☐   Bad ☐   Good ☐   Bad ☐